In memory of my life-long partner, Tadeusz (Teddy) Krecichwost, who loved every living creature, bird and tree as much as I do.

1936-2022

This book is a work of non-fiction. Unless otherwise noted, the author and the publisher make no explicit guarantees as to the accuracy of the information contained in this book and in some cases, names of people and places have been altered to protect their privacy.

WestBow Press books may be ordered through booksellers or by contacting:

WestBow Press
A Division of Thomas Nelson & Zondervan
1663 Liberty Drive
Bloomington, IN 47403
www.westbowpress.com
844-714-3454

Because of the dynamic nature of the Internet, any web addresses or links contained in this book may have changed since publication and may no longer be valid. The views expressed in this work are solely those of the author and do not necessarily reflect the views of the publisher, and the publisher hereby disclaims any responsibility for them.

Any people depicted in stock imagery provided by Getty Images are models, and such images are being used for illustrative purposes only. Certain stock imagery © Getty Images.

ISBN: 978-1-6642-9367-0 (sc)
ISBN: 978-1-6642-9368-7 (e)

Library of Congress Control Number: 2023905217

Print information available on the last page.

WestBow Press rev. date: 04/14/2023

WestBow
PRESS®
A DIVISION OF THOMAS NELSON
& ZONDERVAN

LOGGING

AND

CLEAR-CUTTING

OUR FORESTS, WILDLIFE AND MARSHLANDS ARE DEPLETING,
RESULTING IN LOSS OF SHELTER FOR OUR BIRDS AND ANIMALS

BARBARA ZMIJEWSKI

I dedicate this booklet to all those who love the Canadian outdoors,
who appreciate our forests, our wildlife and the flora and fauna that
rely on trees, marshlands and water for food and shelter.

My hope is that this booklet will encourage readers to do more to help preserve what
remains of our wilderness, watersheds, animals and birds. All of these appear to be
dwindling as a result of widespread de-forestation and housing developments.

Contents

Like many other able-bodied residents of rural Eastern Ontario, I drove a school bus for several years. I enjoyed all of my driving years for Roxborough Bus Lines Ltd., located in Maxville where I first began this job. In my pre-retirement year the company moved to its new location on Hwy. 43 in Avonmore. I retired in June 2019 on the last day of the school year. Covid-19 broke out in Ottawa nine months later, just as the March school break began in 2020.

At the time of writing, September 2022, things are getting closer to 'normal'.

* * * * * *

De-forestation, Clear-Cutting and Wildlife

When I started driving a school bus around December 2012, I found it to be a pleasurable, worthwhile job which covered country roads and highways, towns and villages. While transporting students from villages and farms to school and back home, I would see many forested areas and bushes by the roadside, and a variety of wildlife ranging from deer, wild turkeys and occasionally a ring-necked pheasant with its exotic plumage, along the way.

In the last 3-4 years of driving, and since retiring, I have been quite dismayed at the changes that I've been seeing in the landscape. The scenery has been changing rapidly and dramatically. It is no longer attractive as it was previously. There has been a huge amount of clear-cutting throughout the townships of South Glengarry and North Stormont where I live and travel most. Wooded areas are disappearing fast. There will likely be more treeless fields with the passage of time, as forests are elimitated, to become fields of "cash crops" for large farmers who are looking to make profit. It is horrible to watch. This process is continuing on a daily basis. The scenery in the farming communities is becoming treeless, with piles of recently cut logs, branches and shrubs. More and more trees and bushes, healthy or not, are being felled. Wild animals are dwindling, and some will soon be at risk or become extinct forever. White-tailed deer sightings, for example, have become few and far between since the clear-cutting began. *There is no more shelter for them to hide or breed in.*

During the winter months, the inevitable heavy snow and windstorms make driving along roads with wide-open fields on both sides, challenging for motorists. It is difficult to nagivate safely on open roads which have not been cleared, since the roads have been obliterated by blowing snow after a winter snowstorm.

There have been many occasions during my schoolbus driving years in winter when I had to guess there the road was. I would follow a single pair of tracks made by a previous brave driver in the morning hours before the snowplows had cleared the road. In the meantime, when there are no tracks at all after a heavy snowfall in an open area, it is very easy to miss the road and end up in a ditch. *This is less likely to happen on roads which are wooded on one or both sides.*

Since the logging began, country drives reveal mostly huge open fields with piles of chopped logs. There is little, if any wildlife visible from the roads, and in most agricultural fields, different sized and shapes of machinery can be seen, used mainly to fell trees or to rip the branches off the tree trunks. Also, trees and thickets are being removed to create open spaces for the building of new homes. Developers have continually been constructing roads where new homes are to be built. This is certainly true in the village of Moose Creek, which has been my home for many years. Many new bungalows, cottages and multi-level houses are now standing in areas where forests previously existed, particularly since the pandemic began. Crews continue to fell trees to create roads near the water tower, where I used to glimpse deer, and observe various songbirds.

It is easy to understand the reason for the recent depletion of wildlife here in Eastern Ontario. Lately, only rodents like chipmunks, black or grey squirrels and flying squirrels appear to be plentiful, and they are sometimes fed by local residents. Only occasionally do I see the local white-tailed deer during my daytime travels. I usually spot them at the edge of a rare thicket far afield. These thickets have been diminishing rapidly for the past several years.

I get quite excited when I do see white-tailed deer. They are so beautiful, and graceful when they bolt from danger. In past years, when heavily wooded areas were common, they would occasionally emerge as they searched for food, or a doe and fawn would appear by the roadside waiting for a safe moment to cross the road.

In summertime of past years my partner Teddy and I enjoyed cycling along some of these wooded roads, where stretches of forest still exist. Having witness so much recent destruction of trees on a daily basis, *I can just visualize one day seeing a convoy of tree-removing (ripping) machinery coming along and systematically destroying one healthy tree after another from one of these thickets, in the name of 'progress', from one of these wooded areas, until yet another unattractive, stumpy field with piled-up logs, remains.* I shudder to think that this will probably happen one day, leaving most of North Stormont and the surrounding townships bare and treeless, in the name of profit from "cash crops", or for the construction of more new homes.

I want to mention again, that I have observed machines that, instead of sawing away the branches, will pull until the branches are ripped off the trunk. It is almost unbelievable how, in many cases, the destruction of living trees is performed. *If trees could speak...*

For years I have considered myself a conservationist; therefore, any destruction of nature -- whether it be trees, marshes or wetlands -- or any species of wildlife for whatever reason, is a cause of great concern to me. Therefore, I get very upset when I witness de-forestation or clear-cutting. It destroys wildlife habitat, forcing animals to search further afield to find shelter and food. As a result, animals that sheltered in these areas, such as coyotes or foxes, raccoons and skunks, will approach human habitation in search of an easy meal or to find shelter under someone's porch. *This, after all, was once their habitat, now taken over by humans. They are then considered varmint.*

Coyote Hunters

On one occasion some time ago, while standing in line at the local gas station, I overheard a discussion between two customers regarding the hunting of coyotes. They were commenting about the danger these animals can pose to humans, and that they need to be "harvested". I was getting quite annoyed as I listened to this conversation, particularly since I enjoyed listening to the nocturnal hunting serenades, barks and wails of coyotes some evenings or late at night. I think they are well-organized, intelligent creatures. Since it was clear to these customers that I could hear what they were saying, one of them asked me if I knew that coyotes were dangerous to humans, and if I feared them.

I answered. "There is one thing that I am *really* afraid of: that is, humans with weapons. They can be dangerous and unpredictable. I am not afraid of animals; I respect them, and I give them their space. Coyotes, wolves and other carnivours are highly intelligent. Lately, there seem to be far fewer wild animals in this Township than there used to be, mostly due to hunting and clear-cutting". That comment put an end to their conversation. I completed my transaction at the counter and left the store, feeling pleased about having made this contribution to their discussion.

The night-time barking of coyotes has become less frequent, as de-forestation continues. As I write, new housing construction continues to progess in Moose Creek, at the new Creekside Estates development just outside the village. At this rate, this village will soon become a town. As I mentioned earlier, a huge wooded area has recently been felled by the water Tower. The destruction of timber and the noise of tree-cutting machinery has spooked wildlife away from this area. It appears that the nearest woodland where wild animals might still be found, is the Recreational Trail between Thomas Road and 8th Road. This is a conservation area which, I believe, is off-limits to de-forestation.

Conservation Areas and Clear-Cut Areas

A few kilometers away from the village of Moose Creek is Warwick Forest Conservation Area located not far from Berwick village, which has several kilometres of trails for pedestrians. This is a wild and peaceful place, where I have often visited. Along the trail there is a marshland viewing area a short distance from the highway, with a bench at the end of the wooden walkway for anyone wishing to relax and listen to the bird songs or to view wildlife. Along the trails, I have seen a family of raccoons in a tree, a Snowshoe (or Varying) hare, a full-sized grass snake, and an adult Great Gray Owl sitting on a branch along the trail. We observed each other curiously for quite some time, as I had never seen such an owl in the wild before. There are plenty of woodpeckers as well, along with many different songbirds in the summertime. In the daytime it is a nature-lover's paradise (except in mosquito season). Warwick Forest is also a favourite place for horseback riding. I have met horses on the trails on many occasions.

Recalling the winter of 2013, before the logging commenced, I frequently came across herds of white-tailed deer along the (then) heavily wooded back roads of Apple Hill which was my school bus driving route. As well, returning home from work the previous year from Cornwall, I occasionally came across fox kits playing by the roadside on Tolmies Corners Road; there were also skunks and raccoons scurrying across the road, then disappearing into the deep grass.

One summer's day of that year, returning home from a visit in Greenfield, a village in Glengarry County, my partner Teddy and I decided to drive along a local gravel road on the 5th Concession, where my parents once owned a property. I had not travelled along that concession in quite some time. Along the way, we came upon a massive area that had been clear-cut recently. We were appalled that acre upon acre of an entire forest had been felled. The mounds of recently cut healthy trees, branches and brush were piled high in countless rows. It was one of the largest areas of de-forestation that we had witnessed.

Probably the largest clear-cutting operation that we have seen was in Champlain, Ontario near Vankleek Hill where we had visited a friend. The de-forestation was immense. It was hard to believe that such a huge area of healthy forest had been destroyed in the name of human greed.

Since around 2015, each time that I encountered de-forestation during my travels, I took photographs with my iPhone of the felled trees. The landscape is changing so much...

In recent years, while taking walks around my village, I have stopped to chat with some of the local folks to ask their opinion about this widespread clear-cutting and dwindling wildlife. Most of the people I spoke with, agreed that de-forestation is done for "Greed, not Need".

Apparently farmers can make quite a profit by planting certain crops on their properties, after trees and rocks are removed. If their wooded land is fertile, landowners will use special machinery (as shown on some of my photos) to remove trees and bushes from their land, which is then levelled and "cash crops" are planted. This is becoming a chain reaction. The animals and birds that had sheltered and nested there, must find a home elsewhere. This was what we had witnessed near Vankleek Hill, and in the Greenfield area. It was shocking to see such destruction of our natural resources.

Animals are continually struggling to find food, water, shelter and thickets in which to rear their young. The space for wildlife is getting smaller, while the space needed for development of new homes for our human population, continually increases.

Local Moose Encounters

Several years before my school bus driving days, while travelling by car along Avonmore Road (SDG15) in North Stormont in the fall, I came across several cars parked on the shoulder of the road. The drivers were looking at something across the road, in a farmer's field that was thickly bordered by trees and shrubs. I stopped as well, curious about what there was to see.

Following their gaze, I was amazed to see a cow moose standing in the field, staring at something in the bushes by the road. Soon, a tiny moose calf emerged from the thicket, apparently foraging for food. Both animals appeared to be underweight. It was autumn, and the cow moose and her calf seemed to be having difficulty finding food. I remained at the scene for a while longer, observing the animals, along with the other drivers. It was the first moose cow and calf that I had ever seen in the wild. I have not yet seen an adult bull moose. One of the farmers who was watching the animals, told me that some of the local residents were putting out food for the deer and moose in the area, helping them to survive. Thanks to the efforts on the part of these good people, a small population of moose was still residing in this area.

Later that year, Teddy and I observed an adolescent moose trotting north on the shoulder of Hwy. 138, looking for an opening in the fence that ran along the length of this highway, so as to exit into the shelter of the woodland. As we drove alongside the young moose, the animal found a gap in the fence and vanished into the thicket. It was exciting to observe this young animal until he found safety in the woods.

On another occasion, in the fall of 2011 while passing Larose Forest on our way to Bourget, my partner and I observed two moose calves grazing in a field at the treeline. We parked the car on the shoulder of the road briefly, to observe these beautiful young animals before they too, took cover in the thicket.

On doing some research regarding Larose Forest, I learned that it is a man-made forest, which shelters most of the moose poopulation of this area. These animals favour the cover of deep woods and marshes.

More recently, we were on a car trip to town, on country roads. As I drove along, Teddy was deep in thought. After this spell of silence, he said, "We have not seen any wildlife in this area in a long time. We used to see herds of deer, even the young moose calves, and other animals while driving in the country, both in Quebec and in Ontario. We have seen a lot of wild turkeys, and plenty of livestock on farms, but no *wild* animals." We started to discuss the recent widespread clear-cutting by large farmers in this area. This, we felt, was the probable reason for the sharp decline in wild animal sightings. Many of the animals were probably spooked by logging operations and were deep inside the remaining wooded areas.

Bear Encounters

One summer's evening a number of years ago during a walk by a lake at dusk in Quebec's Eastern Townships, Ted and I heard a grunt, and then a black bear appeared, searching for food in the bushes. Like me, Ted shares a fondness for the outdoors and respect for all living creatures. We were amazed to see a wild bear at close range -- we remained perfectly still. This was a hilly area in South Bolton where I had vacationed as a pre-teenager. Thickets of pine and fir trees were abundant, along with lakes with crystal clear water. Due to the wind direction, the bear did not catch our scent, and kept walking toward the lake.

Later that year a full-grown black bear crossed the road in front of Teddy's car at close range. Ted was driving at a moderate speed, allowing the bear to cross safely. Again, it was a treat for us to see this beautiful animal.

In recent years we have observed an increasing number of wild animals, as well as domestic cats, being struck and killed by speeding drivers. This is a matter of concern to me. Due to my fondness for all species of wild animals, I continually worry about the demise of wildlife. Also, it is very sad that most of the animals that are struck and killed by speeding vehicles while crossing a road, are left lying there, often run over many more times if struck in the centre of a road. It is unfortunate that some drivers have such disrespect for animals.

Deer Crossing

My partner and I recently had a lengthy discussion about an experience that we shared in the Eastern Townships.

This is an incident that occurred more than twenty years ago, when we were leaving South Bolton, Quebec, heading for Montreal after a vacation. It was dusk, and Teddy was driving along a country road that was bordered by coniferous forests in a mountainous area where, in those days, wild animals were abundant. The car in front of us swerved, we heard a loud thud, and the vehicle kept on going. As Teddy proceeded, we saw a large animal lying motionless full length across the road. Teddy drove up to the animal, and stopped the car on the shoulder of the road. We both got out of the car quickly, and cautiously approached the animal. It proved to be a full-grown white-tailed doe in its prime. "What a gorgeous animal!", we commented to each other. I spoke softly to the doe, and gingerly touched its leg. There was no blood visible on the animal or on the road. The doe shuddered and tried to lift its head. It was alive!

As we pondered on how to help this deer, the headlights of other approaching cars could be seen. By now it was dark. We could not allow this beautiful creature to be struck again. Teddy stood in front of the deer, waving his hands to stop cars in both directions; I did the same.

At first the doe lay motionless; then it clawed on the pavement with a hoof. Standing clear of the animal's hoofs to avoid being kicked, I stroked the doe's chest and continued speaking softly to it. Drivers from both directions were stopping. People began to surround us, asking questions about the deer. In a short period of time, there was quite a crowd of onlookers surrounding us and the doe; there must have been twenty persons. The traffic was thus blocked on both sides.

There was a house nearby, away from the road, surrounded by trees. We debated as to whether one of us should approach the house and ask for help. The animal continued to lay on her side, clearly in shock after the collision. As we stood observing the doe, she made a feeble attempt to rise. She tried again and again, and finally she stood up shakily on all four legs. No broken bones! That was a relief. Then, gradually, the deer stepped gingerly toward the trees close to where the house stood. In a moment, the doe made her way into the thicket past the house, and then she disappeared into the forest.

We were all very relieved to see the doe safely on her way. We hoped that she would survive the night and avoid predators.

Teddy and I spoke briefly with some of the onlookers, thanking them for kindly offering their assistance. Soon everyone got into their cars and continued on their way. We did the same. This event was a topic of discussion for us, all the way home. As we travelled, we talked about the possibility of wolves or coyotes stalking the doe in its weakened condition. At that time, as I mentioned earlier, predators were abundant in the Townships. But, all we could do was hope for the best for that doe. We were very happy to know that we had helped save one deer's life by stopping the traffic and giving the animal a chance to escape safely into the thicket. We were also pleased to see that many drivers were ready to help the animal, and to spend the time with the doe to see that she regained the strength to rise on her own, and to seek shelter. This doe was fortunate; the collision could easily have resulted in broken bones or other injury. Who knows how many other animals were not so lucky crossing the busy roads that night.

North Stormont clear-cutting

Tree stumps, Dewar Road,winter 2014

Huge forested are clear-cut near Greenfield in Glengarry County, March 2016

Champlain, Ontario, near Vankleek Hill, massive clear-cutting of forest, September 4, 2016

De-forestation Near Greenfield in Glengarry County, March 2016

Row of felled coniferous trees, 8th Road, North Stormont, Nov. 2015

North Stormont, felled trees, May 2016

Felling of healthy trees, Conc. 5, North Stormont, May 24, 2016

8th Road in North Stormont, tree-stumps, summer 2015

8th Road in North Stormont, summer 2015

Same clear-cut area, Glengarry County, Ontario, March 2016

More stumps on 8th Road in North Stormont, 2015

Clear cutting machine on Tolmies Corners Road

Clear-cutting machine, Tolmies Road in May 2016

This was recently a forest on Tolmies Corners Road in North Stormont, May 2016.

North Stormont, felled healthy trees, Conc. 15, May 2016

Herd of Deer in Eastern Ontario, winter 2015

Winter scene in Eastern Ontario, 2019

Moose Creek Shoreline Restoration, Recreational Park, November 2015

Little lost fawn near Maxville, Ontario, spring 2015. (It was soon reunited with Mom)

Owl's Head, ski resort, the day I was spotted by Bald Eagle, Sept. 2015

Trilliums in North Stormont, Ontario's provincial flower, 2015

North Saskatchewan River, Alberta, summer 2015

IMG 24
Pristine wilderness, North Saskatchewan River, Alberta July 2015

North Stormont trilliums, 2015

Cline River area, Alberta, July 2015

Western Canada, North Saskatchewan River scene, July 2015

Bird of Prey

One autumn day I had an unforgettable experience at Owl's Head, a ski resort near Lake Memphremagog in Quebec. Teddy and I travelled there one weekend to refresh our memories of that beautiful mountainous area where we used to spend many hours doing long-distance cycling. We arrived at the foot of Owl's Head on that cloudless September day, planning to climb as high as we could to enjoy the view and the clean mountain air. The scenery there is very different from the agricultural flatlands of Eastern Ontario.

When we arrived at Owl's Head, Teddy changed his mind about climbing the ski hill as his knee had started to act up. He suggested that I should go ahead alone. I agreed to set off on my own, with my ballcap, binoculars and cellphone, hoping to climb about half-way up. I chose a grassy section of the hill, and began climbing. What with the deep grasses, rocks, stones and potholes, it is hard work to climb this mountain. As I made my way up, I observed many hawks circling around the area. Teddy was still visible down below. We waved to each other and I kept on ascending the steep mountain, huffing and puffing along the way. The scenery become more spectacular with each step I took, as Lake Memphremagog took shape along with the surrounding mountains.

After struggling uphill for a length of time, I felt that I had climbed high enough. I rested for a moment, took photos of my surroundings, then began my descent.

Going downhill was just as difficult as it was climbing up. I had to choose my steps very carefully. I stopped briefly to look around. It was early afternoon, and the sun was nearly above me. Then the sun was blocked as a huge shadow passed under it. I heard a "swoosh" sound up above. Curiously I looked up -- to see, just a few metres above me, a fully mature bald eagle circling and eyeing the small human below it. The feathers on its head and tail were pure white -- and what a large curved, yellow beak it had! The hawks flying nearby were dwarfed by this huge bird of prey. I cringed, feeling small, vulnerable and rather intimidated. It was so magnificent and.... so large! The raptor circled regally above me a few times, and then (thankfully!) it changed course and headed toward another mountain. It must have decided that I was a bit too heavy for it to handle -- I am only 5'4" tall and weighted about 130 lbs. at the time. Perhaps it was just curious. Trying to keep my balance on the steep hill, I grabbed my binoculars and followed the eagle's flight until it disappeared in the distance. Then I continued with my descent. When I finally arrived at the bottom, Teddy told me that he had observed the flight of the eagle, and was concerned that I might have been chosen for its next meal. I was lucky that time.

We chatted with a few of the local folks, and learned that bald eagles have been seen occasionally in this mountainous region. These birds of prey favour thickly forested areas, and they usually nest high up in the tall evergreens.

I would like to mention, however, that about three years ago I spotted an adult bald eagle on several different occasions; one was perched in a local corn field on Tolmies Corners Road in Eastern Ontario where, as I mentioned earlier, the land is quite flat; again, while driving North on Hwy. 138, and also at the Lake of Two Mountains above Hwy. 20, near Montreal. These raptors were not nearly as close to me as the eagle that I witnessed at Owl's Head.

Urban Forest

About thirty or more years ago I lived in an apartment building in Gloucester, south of Ottawa. It was a pleasant place to live, particularly in the summer, with attractive landscaping including a small duck pond. Within 15-20 minutes walking distance from the apartment, was a wide stretch of thickly wooded area near a community called South Keys. The forest consisted of a large variety of broadleaf, coniferous and hardwood trees. I often took walks along the edge of this thicket, feeling as if I were out in the country, with the wind blowing in the trees and the twittering of songbirds. It was a peaceful area that I enjoyed visiting reguarly after returning from work in Ottawa.

One day, during my daily walk along this route, I came upon a large tree-cutting machine that was parked at the edge of the forest. Several trees had already been cut down. A billboard announced a proposed shopping centre in place of the forest! I was totally dismayed to see this. Within the next several weeks many more trees were felled, the songbirds were gone, and more machinery appeared. This clear-cutting upset me so much at the time that, since my job contract was ending, I decided to relocate. In those days finding work elsewhere in my field of work (secretarial) was not an issue; I just wanted to move to some other quiet place, far away from this new development which had destroyed my beloved suburban forest. *Little did I know at the time, how widespread clear-cutting and de-forestation was going to be.*

On my next visit to Ottawa many months later, after having moved away, I drove by the community in Gloucester where I had previously lived. The large wooded area that I remembered was totally gone. It was replaced by a shopping centre, which was well under way. It was massive, with a huge parking lot. Many shops were already under construction. Saplings had been planted along the sidewalk in place of the mature trees that had previously grown there. Of course, traffic had also increased tremendously due to the city's rapidly growing population.

I was relieved to have moved far from this area. However, I was soon to realize that I would experience similar massive destruction of trees in other places where I would live. Clear-cutting and housing developments were occurring both in urban and rural areas; there was no escaping it.

Four-Wheelers and Snowmobiles

So far in this booklet I have been discussing de-forestation and clear-cutting which are, in my mind, the foremost reasons why there are fewer wildlife sightings in rural areas.

There appears to be another cause for the decline of wild creatures in North Stormont: the over-abundance of four-wheelers during the summer months, and of snowmobiles in the winter. Both of these types of noisy machines are being driven in the open fields, wooded areas, on roadways and on village streets at high speeds.

It is understandable that farmers who own many acres of land may find these machines useful throughout the year for searching out lost livestock, or to check out their property for other reasons.

However, both four-wheelers and snowmobiles are extremely annoying to anyone wanting to take a quiet walk in a village or on a country road. They are also guaranteed to spook any animal within a kilometre of the machine. I have encountered many of them (mainly snowmobiles) during the winter while taking my daytime or evening walks. They are very noisy and stress-causing since a pedestrian can never tell when the driver will change his/her course of direction. They often pass very close to pedestrians and probably enjoy intimidating them. I certainly feel that way when a snowmobile or a 4-wheeler is travelling in my direction. Both types of machines generally travel in groups of four or five, so the noise they create is deafening. These machines appear to be used mostly for joy-riding purposes. Wild animals have very sensitive hearing, and must be terrified of 4-wheelers and snowmobiles, which can travel nearly anywhere.

I recall one unusually mild day in January 2016 when I was returning home from a long walk along the Moose Creek Recreational Trail. While walking on the shoulder of the road, I heard behind me the far-away sound of a snowmobile. The noise soon got louder and I nervously looked over my shoulder to see the machine heading at a high speed in my direction. I fully expected the driver to give me some space but he kept heading straight toward me. I had no choice but to step well onto the pavement. As the driver passed me, I saw that he was middle-aged. The look on his face said "Get out of my way or I'll run you over!". I was shaken for quite some time after this event.

An Unspoiled Scenery

Looking back again, to the summer of 2009, I had a wonderful opportunity to travel to Alberta to visit my brother and his family. We travelled in their spacious Motorhome to the North Saskatchewan River in the Canadian Rockies where we stayed for a few days. What a magnificent place to visit! I was in awe of the pristine wilderness and the clean, crisp, dry air of Western Canada. We hiked along some of the numerous trails in the area, which was a camping resort for motorhomes. I expected to encounter a variety of wildlife in this area; however, we saw no animals apart from a few local rodents and birds. This may have been due to the continual roar of sightseeing helicopters above the campground where we stayed. I was rather disappointed not to see any local *wild* animals during my stay there. It was have been a treat to spot an elk, mountain goat or a brown or grizzly bear (from a safe distance). I totally expected to see deer or coyotes along the highway to the North Saskatchewan River from the Edmonton area; however we did see a weasel crossing the road in front of the Motorhome.

I have always been intrigued by woodland animals, particularly timber wolves, and have read several books about these highly intelligent, organized and family-oriented carnivores. I was hoping to perhaps catch a glimpse of these animals or to hear them howling, while visiting the Canadian West.

At the campsite where we stayed during this visit, the sightseeing helicopters that I mentioned earlier, were flying on a regular basis since the day of our arrival. The pilots were offering paying customers a bird's eye view of the incredible scenery below. It was therefore not surprising that we did not spot any eagles or other raptors in the area. They would have been spooked by the chopping noise of the helicopters.

While browsing in the local tourist shop during this trip, I chatted with the shopkeeper who told me that this area was home to grizzly bears, elk, mountain goats and other wildlife. I was fortunate enough, however, to have been able to see the wonderful Canadian Rockies during those few days, and I took many photographs of the spectacular scenery.

Going Paperless

When I first heard about "going paperless", being a tree-lover, I thought it was a wonderful idea. The first thought that came to mind was that I would save countless trees from being cut down if I arranged to receive my monthly bills on my iPhone instead of on paper. This was quite a few years ago.

After several phone calls, I was soon receiving my bills on my cellphone. I found this system to work very well. I imagined that numerous trees would be saved from the logging machines. However, I am really beginning to doubt that any trees are being saved by this "paperless" system. I continue to see more and more bare, open fields where previous forests existed. It seems to me that "going paperless" has no meaning other an having less clutter at home.

During the following summer, while walking along the 8th Road close to where I live, I gasped in disbelief. There was a row of lovely healthy coniferous trees that had been growing in a row by the roadside. *They had been felled and were laying one on top of the other.* This certainly ruined my otherwise pleasant country walk. We all know how many years it takes for trees to grow.

Coyotes in the Night

Recently after dark I heard the sound of coyotes barking their hunting calls. It was reassuring to know that these animals had returned to North Stormont after months of absence. Hopefully they have found shelter in the Recreational Park Conservation area nearby, which is still densely wooded.

Just recently on my way to the village of Avonmore, I noticed an animal running fast across the road several metres away. I wondered if it was someone's dog, or perhaps a wild animal. Driving closer, I was excited to see a full-grown coyote in the open field, close to the road. I stopped the car to observe the animal. It stopped as well, and we stared at each other curiously. The coyote took a few steps toward a near-by forest, but stopped again, to look at me and my car. A few more steps....and again it stopped and looked in my direction. I think the coyote was wondering if it was in danger of being shot at, but it soon concluded that this human was just as curious as the animal itself was. As usual, I thought to myself, "what a lovely creature this is!" The coyote then turned and sped toward the forest at a high speed, tail held between its legs. I stayed to watch the coyote disappear into the woods, and wished it luck and a long life.

* * * * * *

Let's do our best to help preserve what's left of our natural resources, so that our children, and their children, will be able to enjoy the outdoors, fresh air and wildlife. They, in turn, will tell their grand-children about their own outdoor adventures, activities and discoveries. Nature is so important to us all!!

* * * * *

Printed in the United States
by Baker & Taylor Publisher Services